LIGHTNING
BOLT
BOOKS™

The Supersmart Elephant

Mari Schuh

Lerner Publications ✦ Minneapolis

Lerner Publications Company
A division of Lerner Publishing Group, Inc.
241 First Avenue North
Minneapolis, MN 55401 USA

For reading levels and more information, look up this title at www.lernerbooks.com.

Library of Congress Cataloging-in-Publication Data

Names: Schuh, Mari C., 1975- author.
Title: The supersmart elephant / by Mari Schuh.
Description: Minneapolis : Lerner Publications, [2018] | Series: Lightning bolt books.
   Supersmart animals | Audience: Ages 6-9. | Audience: K to grade 3. | Includes bibliographical
   references and index.
Identifiers: LCCN 2017041191 (print) | LCCN 2017054022 (ebook) | ISBN 9781541525313 (eb pdf)
   | ISBN 9781541519848 (lb : alk. paper) | ISBN 9781541527621 (pb : alk. paper)
Subjects: LCSH: Elephants—Behavior—Juvenile literature. | Elephants—Psychology—Juvenile
   literature.
Classification: LCC QL737.P98 (print) | LCC QL737.P98 S395 2018 (ebook) | DDC 599.67—dc23

LC record available at https://lccn.loc.gov/2017041191

Manufactured in the United States of America
1-44320-34566-11/20/2017

Table of Contents

Meet the Elephant

Elephants spend much of the day eating and looking for food. An old female elephant leads a herd of hungry elephants. She remembers where to go.

Elephants are supersmart. They are found in Africa and Asia. Elephants live in forests, grasslands, swamps, and deserts.

This Asian elephant follows a path in the forest.

Smart Elephants

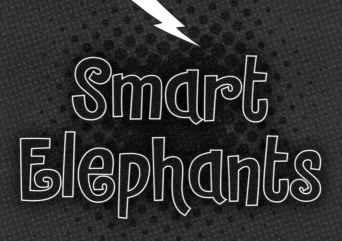

Elephants have great memories. They can remember the best places to find water. They can also remember elephants they knew more than twenty years ago!

Elephants use parts of trees as tools. They scratch themselves with branches. They use twigs to swat away flies.

This elephant is using a stick as a tool.

Elephants work together. They help one another up when a member of the herd falls down. They wait for slower elephants to catch up to the group before moving on.

Elephants also work as a group to keep young elephants safe. Adult elephants form a circle around young elephants to protect them from predators.

These adult elephants are protecting a baby elephant.

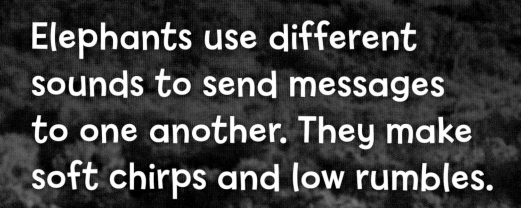

Elephants use different sounds to send messages to one another. They make soft chirps and low rumbles.

Elephants make loud sounds to warn one another of danger.

Sometimes elephants touch each other's trunks when they first meet.

Elephants also communicate through motions. They touch and nudge. They tilt their heads and flap their ears quickly.

The Life of an Elephant

Elephants have big, wide ears and long trunks. Elephants are the largest land animals. These huge animals can weigh more than 7 tons (6.4 t)!

A baby elephant can gain 2 to 3 pounds (1 to 1.3 kg) a day in the first year.

Baby elephants are called calves. Female elephants usually give birth to one calf at a time. Calves weigh about 200 pounds (91 kg) when they are born.

Adult elephants can eat up to 300 pounds (136 kg) of food a day.

Female elephants stay with the same herd their whole lives. The herd roams the land looking for grass, leaves, and fruit to eat. Males leave the herd to live alone or to live with other males.

Elephants begin having their own calves around the ages of ten to fourteen. Elephants in the wild can live sixty years or more.

Elephants in Danger

Elephants are in danger of going extinct. Tigers, lions, and leopards try to eat elephants. People build roads, buildings, and farms on land where elephants live.

Some hunters kill elephants for their meat and skin. But most elephants are killed for their tusks. The tusks are made into jewelry, statues, and other items.

Hunters kill almost one hundred elephants every day for their tusks.

Many people are working hard to keep elephants safe. Laws help protect elephants from being killed for their tusks.

It is illegal in the United States to sell most objects made with elephant tusks.

People are working to protect the land where elephants live. They keep other people from building there. Large national parks give these supersmart animals the space they need to stay around for a long time.

Elephant Diagram

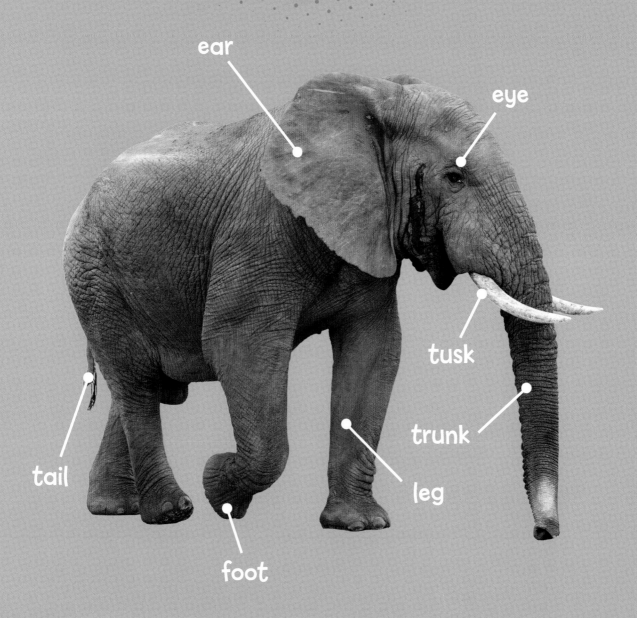

ear

eye

tusk

trunk

tail

leg

foot

Fun Facts

- Elephants can recognize themselves in mirrors. Only people and a few other animals can do this!

- An Asian elephant named Koshik learned to say five words in Korean. He repeated words that he heard people around him saying.

- A group of elephants is sometimes called a parade.

Glossary

communicate: to pass along information

extinct: having died out

herd: a group of animals of one kind

mammal: a warm-blooded animal that breathes air and has hair or fur. Mammals feed milk to their young.

national park: an area of land that is owned by a national government

predator: an animal that hunts and eats other animals

roam: to wander

tusk: a long, pointed tooth

Further Reading

Adams, Avery. *Elephants Work Together.* New York: PowerKids, 2018.

Bell, Samantha S. *Meet a Baby Elephant.* Minneapolis: Lerner Publications, 2016.

KidZone Animals: Elephants
http://www.kidzone.ws/animal-facts/elephants/index.htm

Marsico, Katie. *Elephants Have Trunks.* Ann Arbor, MI: Cherry Lake, 2015.

San Diego Zoo Kids: African Elephant
http://kids.sandiegozoo.org/animals/african-elephant

Science Kids: Fun Elephant Facts for Kids
http://www.sciencekids.co.nz/sciencefacts/animals/elephant.html

Index

Photo Acknowledgments

The images in this book are used with the permission of: mariait/Shutterstock.com, p. 2; JONATHAN PLEDGER/Shutterstock.com, p. 4; worradirek/Shutterstock.com, p. 5; Trevor Fairbank/Shutterstock.com, p. 6; Ian Murdoch/Shutterstock.com, p. 7; Aqua Images/Shutterstock.com, p. 8; Bartosz Budrewicz/Shutterstock.com, p. 9; Rabid Rabbit Photography/Shutterstock.com, p. 10; Brilliant things/Shutterstock.com, p. 11; Riaan Albrecht/Shutterstock.com, pp. 12, 23; Alexey Osokin/Shutterstock.com, p. 13; Quick Shot/Shutterstock.com, p. 14; Claudia Paulussen/Shutterstock.com, p. 15; milka-kotka/Shutterstock.com, p. 16; NurPhoto/Getty Images, p. 17; Peter Fodor/Shutterstock.com, p. 18; Byelikova Oksana/Shutterstock.com, p. 19; Four Oaks/Shutterstock.com, p. 20.

Front cover: Gallo Images-Michael Poliza/Riser/Getty Images.

Main body text set in Billy Infant regular 28/36. Typeface provided by SparkType.